O9-AHW-313

RISE UP

RISE UP WITH A LISTENING HEART
is published by

YORKVILLE PRESS
NEW YORK, NEW YORK

Library of Congress Cataloging in Publication Data
is on file with the publisher.

PHOTOGRAPHS © BY: *Monique Stauder; 30-31, 36-37, 40-41, 54-55, 62-63*
PHOTOGRAPH © BY: *The Monks of New Skete; 80*
ALL OTHER PHOTOGRAPHS BY: *Digital Vision*
DESIGN AND PRODUCTION BY: *Tina Taylor, Dana Magsumbol*

ISBN: 0-9729427-6-9
Printed in Canada by Friesens

Rise Up
with a Listening Heart

Reflecting and Meditating with

THE MONKS OF NEW SKETE

CONTENTS

RISE UP...

INTRODUCTION

Human beings have always wrestled with mystery, and perhaps none has proved so captivating as the question, Is there life after death? Many different religions have offered their response, and so have philosophers and scientists as well. Collectively this has been a lively debate, which seems to have succeeded only in making the question all the more mysterious. Ultimately, there are no sure answers. Whatever choice one embraces will involve some kind of faith. For us as Christian monks, it should be no secret where our faith lies.

Unfortunately, what always seems to characterize the debate is the narrowness of its scope. Resurrection has not to do solely with the afterlife. The word "resurrection" comes from the Greek, meaning "to stand up again, to rise up," and though Christians think of this in terms of belief in the resurrection of Christ — his victory over hell and all manner of death — the word also applies more broadly to the daily moments of rising up that each of us experiences. These reflect the fundamental nobility of life and the ongoing possibility for change and renewal, for personal transformation. As such, rising up involves the most ordinary of realities, whatever someone may or may not believe.

Our hope is that these reflections can become windows into daily life, an invitation to take a second look at the experiences all of us usually take for granted. By deliberately taking time to look at our lives more carefully, more meditatively, we allow a sense of spiritual vitality to arise, often in surprising and delightful ways, and this too becomes both a daily wellspring of gratitude and an ongoing call: Rise up!

RISE UP WITH A NEW DAY

What a wonder each day's sunrise! As soft rays of light peek over the trees, it is always as if for the first time. Dawn beckons with an invitation to begin anew, to see things in a fresh way. "Yesterday is past," it whispers; "you only have today and all its possibilities." Hope rises with the advent of a new day. Part of letting hope spread is to begin each day anchored in stillness, taking nothing for granted, open to whatever the coming day's gift may be. Before you turn on the radio, before you wake the kids, listen to the silence for ten minutes and realize how filled it is, filled with the breath of God! Such silence wants to draw from you a quiet prayer that leans on that presence and seeks to harken to it throughout the day. It all starts with the morning, the fertile soil that helps us realize our vow always to be better, to leave our world a better place by day's end.

RISE UP
AMIDST LIFE'S ABUNDANCE

Moments of daily renewal are like seeds that sprout and burrow deep into the soil of our inner life. No matter how passing, how insignificant such moments may seem, they connect the whole of our life together. If we pay attention we can feel our lives as a free and irrepressible melody of hope. Such moments are as close as a shaft of sunlight breaking through the morning mist, or a red-tailed hawk serenely catching an updraft and then allowing itself to be launched across the vast expanse of the sky. Such magic at only the price of our attention! No need to grasp greedily at such moments: They come upon us naturally — yes, repeatedly — in the utter simplicity and fullness of life. There is more than enough for us all.

RISE UP WITH MUSIC 1

What can soothe the soul as much as the grace of music? Music allows us to express and deal with our feelings constructively, lifting them to a new place, a new level of integration. Whether our feelings at the moment are joy, sorrow, or even heartache, the enchantment of music helps free the soul to sing, and its energy becomes an infectious catalyst to change. *On the wings of a beautiful melody, suddenly we feel different, ready to move forward.* No doubt this is why classical music is such a natural for the start of the day: It clears our head and brings us to a calm center. Surprisingly, this can even take place in your car. With today's astonishing advances in sound quality, rush hour can suddenly become a front row seat at symphony hall, letting you arrive at work focused and ready to do your best. All you need do is open yourself to its enrichment.

*R*ISE UP IN THE MORNING

Awakening for a non-morning person takes some rising up. Before the muscles can be goaded to stir the limbs, the ears can help. In early spring and before dawn, just before shapes are sure, a single bird tunes up an almost cacophonous chorus. Not yet — they will die down. Next the hummingbird, nature's buzzing alarm. A cardinal or robin can bring a smile; a nattering chipmunk or piercing crow can be a razor to the sleepy brain. Almost time now. The dog is restless, waiting for your first blink.

Okay, look up; is that a beam of sun? Here comes the wet nose, perhaps a paw or two. A dog's enthusiasm is contagious; it may take a minute or two, a micro prayer, a quick review of what awaits. Arms over the head and expand the lungs, smell the new. Now twist and hit the floor. It's a parable of life. *You can't expect much if your feet aren't on the ground, physically and spiritually. Get on with life.*

*R*ISE UP FROM TEMPTATION

Rarely do we conceive of temptation as a stimulus to virtue, yet often its presence signals that we are doing something right in our life. When we channel our energies in positive directions, the hidden, shadow side of our nature will awaken and offer us fierce resistance and whisper temptations of all sorts. Take that as an opportunity: We need not fall for it. *Temptations are normal and, though challenging, they have a chance of helping us along the pathway to inner freedom.* The temptation to cheat on a spouse, for example, far from being a betrayal, can be the occasion for a deeper choice of one's mate and can actually stir us on to strengthen the relationship if we face it honestly. Acknowledging the temptation consciously is the first step towards dealing with it and not letting it control us. Although each of us intimately knows occasions when we fell victim to temptation's sneaky assault, such is the stuff of being human. By encouraging in us a broader perspective, such moments keep us humble while at the same time challenging us to meet the next occasion of temptation with greater self-possession and integrity.

Rise up WITH GOOD READING

When we consider sources of re-creation, perhaps none is so close at hand as reading. Whether it be the classics or modern mysteries, reading helps form and re-form us. Fortunate indeed are we when we recognize the power of words and take care what we put in our line of sight. Selecting good literature not only nourishes the soul, it sparks new thoughts and possibilities and ever inspires us to become better human beings. Why feast on hours of television when some of the most insightful reflection ever crafted by human beings lies as close as your bookshelf? Take the time. *Good literature engages the whole person, body, mind, and spirit*, and lets us enter into intimate dialogue with perennial masters whose thought never dies. By reading and re-reading their words, we make them partners in our journey, helping us rise to more abundant life.

Rise up WITH BEAUTY

Moments of beauty easily lead us to pray when we are awake to their presence: a full moon illuminating a soft winter landscape, or a van Gogh celebrating an immortal starry night. Outside, inside, it does not matter for one who beholds beauty. We stand transfixed, drawn in wonder to the beautiful sight or sound, thought or touch, and what it displays. Is this a prayer that arises spontaneously, this movement that invites us to deeper, more intimate seeing? We lose ourselves in a glimpse of what the theologian and mystic Gregory of Nyssa described:

"The whole of creation is but one single temple of the God who created it."

Dare we believe this? We have only to be still, to linger awhile and look out at the stars in our own backyards and listen to what stirs within us. Listen. Can moodiness and short-temperedness withstand the sight of a red-breasted grosbeak alighting on a feeder, delighting in its meal? The heart awakened by beauty is captivated, engaged by a presence it naturally responds to in the simplicity of prayer.

"Nothing would remain stable in human society if we determined to believe only what can be held with absolute certainty." — *St. Augustine*

RISE UP THROUGH FAITH

Faith is much more than belonging to a particular religion or believing in specific doctrines. In fact, it is less a noun, a "thing" we either have or don't have, than an action, a way of being. Its fundamental energy pulses throughout human life and provides us with the confidence to move forward, no matter what we might be feeling. What a relief to understand that we are not bound to such vagaries, that true faith transcends them all, and can be present even when we're most uncertain of its content. Surprise! *As people of faith, we can be at peace with this mystery, and still acknowledge faith's reality at the core of our values, our choices.* We can draw from its strength, facing both the joyous and the tragic elements of life honestly, without ever surrendering to hopelessness and despair. For there, deep inside ourselves — deeper than all doubt — is a "Yes!" to life, to life that is utterly grounded in the Divine goodness and that is destined for glory.

*R*ISE UP WITH KINDNESS

A kind person — a virtuous person. Between them, there is a big difference. A kind person is kind because he or she accepts people as they are, covers them with kindness. Kindness is beautiful, the most beautiful thing on this earth. Virtuous people are activists, obsessed with the desire to impose their principles and goodness and easily condemning, destroying, hating. . . . In this world there is a lot of virtue, and so little kindness.

— Father Alexander Schmemann

What is the experience of kindness? It is time spent with another: listening, walking, sitting, working, playing, singing — it is a heart always inclined towards the other. Kindness connects people; it does not isolate. Kindness emerges through concern for, consciousness of, engagement with, or giving space to another. It rises up to meet the other.

Kindness surfaces unexpectedly. It is like a mist, a cloud, a wave, a fragrance, a gentle breeze, a melody; it is a song, a smile, a chuckle that draws us in and envelops us.

It cannot be captured; it can only be given away.

RISE UP

FROM LOW SELF-ESTEEM

The image makers of this world parade before us visions of life and health that are ever young, ever successful, clothed in a seamless tapestry of cheerfulness and glee. The mirror on the wall portrays a vision with many more blemishes. Measured against popular standards, we can easily undervalue our own worth. But the diary of daily life is a drama of infinite variations of both joy and frustration. ***To be whole is to be perfectly human, with all its vitality and weaknesses.*** The judge of that perfection is the Higher Power who sees into our hearts and who knows our nature and loves us, no matter what. To measure up to our own standards is an inhuman task, so leave that judgment to a Higher Power. Rise up to the life we are all called to: to be perfectly human as the Creator intended, just as all the other living beings with whom we share this world are perfect in their intended way.

RISE UP WITH GOOD WORK

At a time when so many experience their work as a necessary evil, how heartening it is to meet individuals whose work manifests enthusiasm and vitality, who are able to stay positive even when they'd rather be doing something else. Surprisingly, they are not simply the lucky few who have managed to get paid for doing something they enjoy. Rather, they've learned that any task, *any job, can be transformed by the attitude that we bring to it,* and that we can grow even in the most unappealing of circumstances. Who we become is the result of engaging with life. If we do so wholeheartedly, creatively striving to do the best we're capable of, we'll experience both the satisfaction that comes with doing good work, and its fruit: ever-deepening maturity. That's true whether we're cleaning the house or designing software, mowing the lawn or teaching physics. While we'll always look for work that reflects our passions and interests, there is great comfort in knowing that no task is unredeemable and that *the manner in which we carry out all our work has a direct bearing on our spiritual health.*

RISE UP WITH A GOOD MEAL

Often we think of growth and renewal in elevated terms that can cause us to miss inspiration that is closer at hand. As important as it is to dream and set goals that will engage us over many years, we also need to infuse daily life with more modest experiences that energize us and keep us moving in a positive direction. One of the most accessible human experiences is a good meal, both from satisfaction in preparing it and from joy in sharing it. When we approach the meal as the sacred experience that it is, we discover that spirituality is hardly grim, and that lessons of the spirit can come in the most sensuous of settings. So make cooking part of your spiritual discipline. Instead of throwing something together at the last minute, take some time at the start of the week to plan your meals. Consider who will be sharing them, and let your care be transparent in the way you shop and in the manner of your preparation. Let yourself delight in it all — colors, smells, flavors, presentation. All of this becomes your gift to those whom you love. Finally, be grateful as you eat. Savor the moment and give it its due. *A good meal engages all our senses, tying us to reality, making us taste life's essential goodness.* Why would we ever want to rush that?

RISE UP FROM SELF-DOUBT

Self-doubt descends like a cold, gray day. Another day lost. To start over is only to begin the cycle again — it's the same old story. Successive failures bite at self-confidence like a bitter wind slapping your face when you open the door to head out into the cold morning. The only question: What else can go wrong? Something, no doubt! But why? *Every moment and every event are part of life's journey — none are wrong.* Each one sheds new light on a personal story that is unique. A failure simply opens a new avenue to explore. To make a mistake is to build knowledge, to expand our horizons in different directions. Even having to start over is rising up to a new beginning. It's a resurrection in the truest sense. This is why we can say our strength is shown through our weakness. You cannot rise down. You can only rise up.

Rise up WITH CREATIVITY

Creativity is more expansive in our lives than we realize. Often we can sell short our creative talents simply because we're not landscape painters or budding novelists, and this can leave us feeling vaguely inadequate and ordinary. But how this changes if we think about creativity creatively, honestly accepting the many and varied ways it expresses itself in our lives. Creativity is what distinguishes us. Each of us interacts with life in our own distinctive way, and there is enormous joy in discovering that the work of art we're creating through our activity is ourselves. From choosing the clothes we wear to decorating our house, from designing the garden to growing a business, from deepening our friendships to laying out a Web page, *creativity reflects our uniqueness and infuses energy and spirit into life.* Creativity plays with the possible, and when we are being creative we feel fully alive and vibrant, celebrants at the liturgy of life. So look to yourself and feel the possibilities, think of what can be and follow your path with zeal and dedication. No greater joy is known to human beings than the satisfaction that comes with creatively becoming who we are meant to be.

"No matter how often defeated,
you are born to victory.
The reward of a thing well done
is to have done it."

— *Ralph Waldo Emerson*

RISE UP WITH PERSEVERANCE

Looking for renewal in our lives, sometimes we miss the obvious: where our real passion and love lie. Grace is present there. How easy it is to follow other people's scripts, busying ourselves with books and seminars detailing how we should become fulfilled and renewed — and all the while ignore what really energizes us. Why are we so afraid of following our deepest passion? Perhaps we fear failing. When we have our as-yet-unrealized ideal, at least it still exists as a possibility. We can always comfort ourselves with the tonic of our dreams. But once we try, and fail . . . often it is our deepest hopes that burst into flames as well.

So? The call still echoes. *Believe in your dreams, in yourself.* We can always try again, with renewed effort and zeal. We can learn from past mistakes and set our sights ahead once again. That movement, in whatever context we are called, allows us to grow in unanticipated ways. We can strive for greatness, and with it real integrity. The crucial point is never to lose hope. Hope allows us to accept the risk of committing all our energies to what gives us life, confident that wherever it leads us will be worth the effort.

"HAPPY ARE THEY WHO LIVE IN YOUR HOUSE,
THEY SING YOUR PRAISES ALL DAY LONG.
HAPPY THE PILGRIMS WHO FIND THEIR
STRENGTH IN YOU, WHO SET THEIR HEARTS
ON REACHING YOU."

Psalm 84: 4,5

*R*ISE UP THROUGH WORSHIP

Deep within our hearts is an impulse to worship, to lift the whole of who we are in a deeply personal act of gratitude and wonder. Worship arises as a response to realizing that our life is a gift, and reflects what is most basic and noblest in us. While true worship is free and spontaneous, worship also calls us to something deep and universal, and in its swell we feel embraced by a loving presence. Such an experience, ineffable and unmerited, creates an even deeper desire to respond, to let our life become a continuous movement of praise and thanksgiving. This need not be confined solely to church, synagogue, or mosque. It seeks to be at the heart of a rhythm that beats through the whole day — from the moment we open our eyes until we turn off the light at day's end. When we get in touch with that impulse and see how naturally it expresses itself, we'll find ourselves mouthing "thank you" at the least indication of grace. It is difficult to conceive of living life in any fuller way.

"We never know how high we are
till we are called to rise
and then, if we are true to plan
our statures touch the skies."
— *Emily Dickinson*

Rise up FROM DEATH

It is entirely human to try to look beyond the limits of our life to that moment of death beyond which is nothing but darkness and mystery. We cannot pierce it. We wonder, at times anxiously, at times bravely, hoping for a definitive insight, but we're never sure of death's secrets. Only by faith can we live with such ambiguity, and even here it is an uneasy truce. What can help us is to notice the series of daily deaths we all undergo throughout our lives — those errors in judgment and moments of alienation, the hurt feelings and careless words, a sense of desolation — and reflect on what always seems to follow: Death never has the last word. In that dark stillness comes a summons; a quiet call stirs from the depths of who we are: Rise up! *Rise up to new life, to a new vision of who we can become!*

RISE UP WITH A LISTENING HEART

In the wake of growth and renewal, we have a chance to experience a new sensitivity to the needs of others. Though blatant human suffering usually doesn't escape notice, subtler forms often go undetected: those who are always cut off as they try to express their feelings; the distress a friend tries to hide when you ask how things are going at home. How such moments can pass just below our conscious awareness! What is most often needed from us isn't all that dramatic: a listening heart. *In listening to the other – really listening – we offer a gift that is increasingly absent in our culture.* So many of us today can feel isolated, alienated, for the simple reason that we don't experience ourselves being listened to or accepted for who we really are. What a switch it is to offer that to another with no strings attached, and to witness the grace of someone suddenly coming to life because of it.

Rise up WITH MUSIC 2

Given its primal attraction and power, it is no surprise that there is a link between music and religious experience. *Music gives access to the heart's deepest emotions, bringing them to light in a natural flowering that creates a deep sense of unity and peacefulness.* Sacred chants, in all their varieties in the great religious traditions of the world, have been shown to physically alter the consciousness of the listener, planting peace and quiet

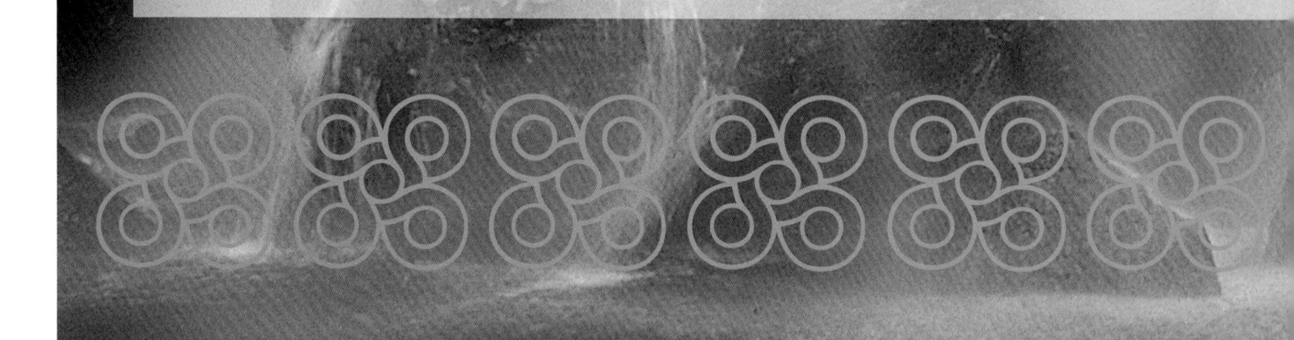

attentiveness. This is why so many people find listening to chant beneficial, even those who are not formally religious. It matters not whether we understand the meaning of the words; the melodic rhythms support and interpret the music's meaning in their own right, taking us to levels of understanding beyond what words can tell. If you value tranquillity and inner calm, leave room in your music library for a body of sacred chant, and don't be hesitant to seek refreshment in its haunting praise.

RISE UP FROM LONELINESS

There is a radical difference between loneliness and aloneness. Loneliness tends to drift into self-pity, making us ill at ease with ourselves and tempted to use others simply as a means of relief. Aloneness, on the other hand, is more constructive. Although it flourishes in solitude, aloneness provides the basis for true relationship and friendship. Aloneness is able to receive others on their own terms, freely, because it doesn't crave them. It accepts them as they are. Further, being truly alone means that we're able to stand our own company. We can believe in the love others offer us, and thus we don't need to fret when we're called to be alone for a time. Indeed, aloneness becomes restorative, a time to lean more deeply on God's supportive presence. Loneliness is an entirely human emotion that we'll experience from time to time, but we need not accept it like a prison sentence. By calming ourselves and getting some perspective, *we can know an aloneness that carries with it real peace.*

RISE UP WITH LAUGHTER

The joy of laughter is immensely contagious and therapeutic, reflecting a deep engagement with life that delights in paradox and the zany side of things. From Charlie Chaplin to Monty Python to Dilbert, genuine humor offers its own wisdom, and has its rightful place in the treasure house of graceful living. Life is serious, but it need not be taken too seriously. More than almost anything else, an insightful and healthy sense of humor is a defiant response to life's absurdities and challenges. Laughter carries within it an energy that seizes despair and casts it overboard, re-establishing inner balance and calm. *Through its own infectious rhythms, laughter spreads healing as a gift both for ourselves and for others.* Be grateful for those who make you laugh — theirs is a ministry that keeps us healthy.

"Heaven is under our feet
as well as over our heads."
— *Henry David Thoreau*

RISE UP IN NATURE

Why is it that so many of us seek connection and solace in nature? It is an impulse that goes beyond the universal need for relaxation and moves in the direction of meaning, of being in communion with all living things. We are drawn to the natural world to recover a sanity hyperactivity mocks, to recapture a stability we hope will become the context for a new inner freedom. In its sanctuary of silence, nature speaks its own gentle word, a word that soothes the anxiety and restlessness of our hearts. Its beauty offers endless variations on a theme of hope, infusing in those alert to its melody a determination that is grounded in peace. But we must make time for this. Start by taking advantage of simple opportunities that life provides you with: A half hour in the garden does wonders for the stress of the past day; a walk in the park or woods with a pair of binoculars offers easy entry into the fascinating world of birds; a walk along a lake or ocean enlivens our spirit and quiets our mind. *There need never be an end to our courtship of nature — all it requires is our presence.*

RISE UP AND DO NOTHING

It is not hard to believe that sometimes people are so busy they can't even go on vacation. Must the car run out of gas before we fill the tank again? Paradoxically, the word "vacation" comes from the Latin *vacare*, which means "to be empty". What happens on vacation is the necessary process of emptying ourselves of our many concerns. It facilitates an essential distancing from our everyday lives that allows us to physically and psychically relax and obtain perspective to see how we can live more authentically and faithfully. Viewed in this way, a vacation is less a luxury than a vital touchstone to our deepest reality. So take a week with no other task than to relax and enjoy yourself. You'll see the power in doing nothing. Whether it be at the shore where waves soothe your consciousness, or hiking through a national forest and being enfolded by the silence, such breaks help us recover an essential dimension of ourselves that can be lost in busyness. *The rest and relaxation, the change of pace and place, let our imagination catch its breath and play a crucial role in the renewal of the self.*

"It is more important to remember God than it is to remember to breathe."

— *St. Gregory of Nazianzus*

*R*ISE UP IN DAILY LIFE

Planting yourself squarely in the present moment is a condition for being truly alive and happy. How easy it is to dwell on the promise of the future — the long-awaited vacation, the promotion, the anniversary — and overlook the significance of more common moments that arise each day, indeed each hour. Our personal rebirth begins here and now, one frame at a time. Take time to notice. A freshly brewed cup of coffee that we savor in silence, an invigorating shower that rinses away the past night's sleep — these are but two examples of daily rites that have the power to lift our spirits and carry us forward through the day. What counts in these routines is our awareness of them. We can go through such moments on automatic, or we can discipline ourselves to pay attention to them with a spirit of openness and gratitude. Keep track of yourself today and see if this is not true: *Life feels so different to the one who takes time to notice it.*

"BEHOLD, I DO NOT GIVE LECTURES
OR A LITTLE CHARITY.
WHEN I GIVE, I GIVE MYSELF."
— *Walt Whitman*

Rise up WITH GOODNESS

The capacity for human goodness reveals itself in so many dramatic ways we can overlook its more ordinary manifestations: the smile that carries with it no agenda, the word that soothes a broken spirit, the thoughtful act that comes upon us when we least expect it. All of us are debtors to goodness — every day, every hour. Can we slow ourselves down enough to receive its gifts, to become conscious of the significance concealed in their simplicity? For no matter how apparently unremarkable such incidents may be, they have the capacity to lift our hearts and to inspire us to make better use of our energies as well. *By allying ourselves with the wide scope of goodness — wherever it appears — we become one more sure link in a collective rise of consciousness that benefits us all.*

RISE UP
FROM LOSING A FRIEND

The loss of a friend after decades of friendship leaves a deep and lasting hole in the soul. The way to rise up from such a depth is to let the separation give new perspective to the rarity of such a gift. Let the bond that filled the years roll out like a receding tide revealing small and varied treasures: shells and sand dollars, those individual likes and interests shared and gradually absorbed, one for art and travel, the other for food and music; a shark's tooth of humor; the flotsam of life's twists and turns; smooth, shining pebbles chattering of multicolored memories; and there, almost hidden in glistening seaweed, a pearl of joy, a mystery deeper than the ocean — *the awareness that an intimacy enriched by the shared pull and draw of what is of the Spirit is not gone but endures,* even now, to be perfected in the life to come.

*R*ISE UP WITH EXCELLENCE

How important to note the effect excellence has on the human condition! *Simply put, excellence inspires.* No matter the particular way it expresses itself, witnessing excellence stirs within us a desire for it in our own lives, and the determination to realize it. Ask anyone who excels in a chosen field, and they will always speak of someone they initially looked up to, who fired their imagination, who encouraged them to give their very best, and whose own example served as a catalyst for that process.

Where would we be without such examples? Is not the power of the Olympics manifest in each athlete's commitment to excellence, and is that not a gift for us all, inspiring us to do our best as well? When we attend a special exhibit of a famous artist, does not its quality reinforce our own commitment to realize excellence in our own lives? Or when we become aware of the moral stature reflected in organizations such as Doctors Without Borders or the AIDS hospice programs of HOPE worldwide, is it possible for our ideals to be unaffected? By its very reality and attractiveness, excellence challenges us to achieve it in our own lives by always giving our best, one step at a time. The key is never to give up; let the vision carry us as far as we are capable.

"You gain strength, courage and confidence
by every experience in which you really stop
to look fear in the face....
You must do the thing you cannot do."
— *Eleanor Roosevelt*

Rise up FROM FEAR

A decision avoided again. The past too present. Dry throat, panting, sweat droplets forming on the brow. Those nasty little zeros of light caused by nerves in the eyes darting across the field of vision. Everything in the room looks familiar and yet distant. The mind will not focus. A line read and then re-read still does not sink in. No distraction is strong enough to obliterate the nagging worry about making that move, taking that step, breaking through that boundary. Looming like a thundercloud in the distant sky drifting ever closer: the moment of truth. Then, a gentle tap on the shoulder and a familiar voice asks: *"Are you ready to go?" Leaden legs twitch, fidget; then, a deep breath, a sigh; adrenaline begins to flow, a slide forward, and you rise up to go. "Yes!"*

RISE UP TO THE ROAR OF THE OCEAN

Your feet are throwing sand up your back as you race down the shore straight out towards the water. Splash! Swoosh! You're in. You pull the water past you with each stroke as you head out to the spot where you guess the next wave will break, giving you the perfect ride in. The glassy blue-green water swells and rises, pulling strength away from the shore and gathering it back in from the deep beyond. This is it; you turn towards the shore, first hesitating, then frantically swimming, trying to get onto the wave at just the right moment. The rolling wave breaks under you but you're at the crest, surveying the beach below, feeling the power of the crashing wave, ears bombarded by the roar of the ocean surf. Then you hit the shore, plunge into the broken wave, tumbling to the sand, leaping up in the shallow water.

It's life! Riding over the turmoil below, soaring towards your dream, then the crash of conflicting realities, but you burst through, rising up for the next challenge.

RISE UP WITH GOOD READING 2

There is a way of reading that emphasizes depth over breadth, savoring over speed, wisdom over facts. Often referred to in monastic tradition as *lectio divina* — sacred reading — it is a pursuit that allows the text to become an active partner in our own transformation through repetition and quiet reflection. By staying with a passage that speaks to us, we will find it working within our depths, bringing light to our souls, warmth to our hearts. Reading in this way — slowly, leisurely, meditatively — is the productive cultivation from which real personal change occurs. Try it and see if it is not true. Instead of digesting all your reading at a gallop, save for yourself at least ten minutes a day for intense reflection on one passage. Chew it, savor it, without care for moving on. *You will be delightfully surprised at all the connections it elicits and the new depth with which you understand it.*

"Neither death nor life, no angel, no prince,
nothing that exists, nothing still to come,
not any power, or height or depth,
nor any created thing, can ever
come between us and the love of God . . ."

St. Paul's letter to the Romans 8:38-39

RISE UP FROM SPIRITUAL DOLDRUMS

There are times in life when a spiritual sirocco sets in. The bitterness in the world or one's personal life gives a toehold to a cynicism, a doubt: What's it all coming to? Is warfare so endemic to the human condition, between nations or cultures or religions or classes or families, that my puny efforts to find peace, even in my own inner space, are doomed? Are Cain and Abel and Judas inevitable?

Or, is it easier to shift the burden to the perennial questions: Where is God? Is God angry? Do I limp like Jacob with sciatic neuralgia and cry foul?

But then, in the midst of the sweaty struggle, a breeze of faith cools the heart, like dew in the desert. Beyond my questions, deeper than my doubts, I feel nevertheless that I am loved, understood, and that makes all the difference. I am free to trust, to believe that God is free, and in fact chooses to be at home with our mortal weakness and in our creaturely brokenness, more keenly than in our piety and virtue.

So, rise up, my soul, and sing Paul's hymn:

RISE UP FROM EVIL

No more courageous and inspiring example of the human spirit exists than the seemingly spontaneous emergence of goodness on the heels of evil. Whatever form it may take — the generosity of heart in the aftermath of 9/11, the stirring of conscience that labors for human rights, the giving of relief to those victimized by war and violence, to name but a few — such acts of mercy and self-sacrifice defy evil's dark foreboding. Their sheer transparency lets us see what lifts the hopes of all, making us believe once again that goodness really is stronger than the very worst evil can hand out, that ultimately it can triumph over every shade of darkness. This is the rationale for pursuing goodness in the face of evil. Such is the tireless example of each person who labors for the good for goodness' own sake, who elevates life and vanquishes cynicism through the power of love. Whenever this is seen, in whatever context, hope arises and becomes infectious for us all, granting new confidence that is stronger than despair.

"The deepest feeling
always shows itself in silence."
— *Marianne Moore*

Rise up WITH SILENCE

Ours is an age that is increasingly uncomfortable with silence. For all the wonder of technology and new forms of communication, one gets the feeling that cell phones, television, home entertainment centers, and e-mail are often merely diversions, tools to distract us from the gnawing sense of poverty we feel within. Silence frightens us because it makes that poverty palpable, and this in turn leads us to seek refuge in noise, which ultimately is no balm for the emptiness we can't fill.

Silence need not have such an edge, but we have to give it a chance. Embraced with courage, it affords us the chance to be mindful of God's abiding presence while staying grounded in our best selves. *Silence allows us to be conscious of our own thoughts and to choose our own way with care, essentials to real happiness.* See what happens when you make time for silence at the beginning of the day: Just ten minutes of silent attentiveness will order your thoughts and focus your mind, making your life fertile soil for the coming day.

RISE UP
WITH A LIVE PERFORMANCE

It doesn't have to be Carnegie Hall or Tanglewood: A chamber group on a Vermont mountain, or a folk trio on a grassy oxbow of the Batten Kill in upstate New York, or anywhere in the world where performers engage us in their art, a resurrection is at work. Despite the perfection of CDs, live music makes the difference, akin to the difference between seeing great art in a book and standing in the presence of the original.

Live is just that, and it beckons us to respond not just with the senses and the aesthetic area of the brain, but with the heart. Performers work together to make something wonderful — you can see the mystery in their eyes, the shared pride and joy of life. The sway of a cellist or nodding head of a pianist, the heave of a flutist's chest speaks that each has entered in to their work and become art. A responsive audience feels it and rises up to applaud.

The chant that fills our church invites no clapping hands but a soaring spirit in both singer and worshipper, which can seem to defy gravity and lift one into the sacred space beneath the dome.

In all of this there is an interior rising up, a gravitational pull to the good, the true, the beautiful. *This is the nobility of our humanity, a reflection of the Divine.*

"Grace strikes us when we are in great pain and restlessness....
Sometimes at that moment a wave of light breaks into our darkness,
and it is as though a voice were saying: 'You are accepted.'"

— *Paul Tillich*

RISE UP FROM ILLNESS

Yes, it is important to do whatever we can to stay healthy, but when sickness or injury does come, it is helpful to see it as an opportunity to grow. It is not simply "down" time (though that may be necessary, too). Illness is a great teacher. Even though it is not easy to sit willingly at its feet and listen to its wisdom, its lessons are poignant and crucial. How many people have said that dealing with a serious illness was one of the most significant experiences of their lives, a gift that helped transform them into someone utterly new? *An illness throws our vulnerability and mortality in our face, challenging us to accept the gift of life in a fresh way and to recognize the miracle of each day.* We can ignore this, let it crush us, or let its reality galvanize our inner resources, leading us to do whatever we can to get better. With such an attitude we discover and proclaim what it means to be truly human.

RISE UP THROUGH FORGIVENESS

Perhaps nothing so weighs down the spirit as the sadness engendered by broken relationships. It becomes the lens through which we see everything, invariably tarnishing whatever our eyes rest upon. So much beauty passes by unacknowledged simply because we're caught in our own melancholy, our own depressing sense of alienation.

But how things change the moment we experience a shift, when life reveals the possibility of a new beginning that is sincere and open. Is it worth the risk? That question is perhaps best answered by our own experience, when another offered us forgiveness when we deserved nothing. Could we bear now to live without that?

Forgiveness believes in the human capacity to change. It offers each of us the opportunity of reclaiming higher ground by giving another person the chance to become someone new. While one of the most precious gifts we can offer another, the effect forgiveness has on us is equally dramatic: Suddenly our world feels different, unhindered by our need to keep the other in lockup.

The Monks of New Skete are an Eastern Orthodox monastic community in Cambridge, New York. They began in 1966 and support themselves by breeding and training dogs at their monastery, and by making and selling specialty foods. They are the authors of **I & Dog, In the Spirit of Happiness: Spiritual Wisdom for Living**, *and their best-selling guides to dog training,* **How To Be Your Dog's Best Friend** *and* **The Art of Raising a Puppy**; *and they've produced an award-winning video training series,* **Raising Your Dogs With the Monks of New Skete**, *and a wall calendar,* **The Monks of New Skete Celebrate Dogs.**
For additional information, visit their website at www.newsketemonks.com.